Three Times

Around the World

~

Donna Allard

Three Times Around the World

Cover design: Donna Allard & Ronda Wicks
Edited by Ronda Wicks

Indexed.

Library and Archives Canada Cataloging in Publication

Author: Donna Allard (1956-)

ISBN: 978-0-9738671-7-6

First edition

river
bones
press

Award winning poet Donna Allard was raised in the fishing village of Richibucto, New Brunswick, Canada, which must surely lend to her hardy spirit and well seasoned pen. Allard's soulful eye captures the impact of light on the lens of a camera just as masterfully as she paints with words. As stated in a review by Sky Wing Press publisher Ronda Wicks Eller.

Achievements:
2019 International Beat Poet Laureate
National Beat Poet Foundation Inc.,CT, USA
2016 Nominated for the Writers' Trust Fellowship Award

Published Works:
2019 SkyWing Press, Cold Fire ISBN 975-1-9990964-4-1
2019 River Bones Press, Three Times Around the World
ISBN 978-0-9738671-7-6
2013 Broken Jaw Press, From Shore to Shoormal
ISBN 978-1-55391-111-1

* Cover image Royalty free.

Three Times
Around the
World

~

Donna Allard

This book is inspired by years of living in a small
rum-runner village, situated on the ocean's coastline where
foggy summer night ghosts tarry by the boardwalk. They
whisper about days of old and long lost sailors who set out to
sea. "Three times around the world", they say, with a deep
rooted smell of tobacco as the salty
air fades into the night heralding,
"Around the world one more time!"

Memories

sailing to

forgotten

islands...

Heartfelt thanks

to the

National Beat Poet Foundation Inc., CT, US.

Brian Stevens

and everyone

who supported me throughout the decades

~~~~~~~~~~~~~~~~

Index

Three Times Around the World

Three Times Around the World

three times around the world:
flowing memories swallowed
resemble a Sahara mirage--
your thirst marked out
by old footprints left
as thinking pools

Along the Saint Ann Shore I

along the Saint Ann Shore
I think of my father;
whose hands made sandcastles
from which I built a world
where tidal waves rush
and carry me along,
but I am rock. This coast
is a whale at feeding time,
a roar that consumes me--
but I am a rock."

Along the Saint Ann Shore II

along the Saint Ann Shore
I think of my mother's reminder:
"don't forget to get ice cream cones".
father nodded and I yelled "YES!"
she warned me about jellyfish &
father nodded again.
"I'm not afraid", I replied.
we ate ice cream and watched
the sun melt into Napoleon--
the tides swam away
along the Saint Ann Shore

Dead Man's Beard

in my youth I would venture far and wide
by foot or bicycle

down tall grass pathways,
down rocky shorelines,
into nearby woods

where bears, moose and lynx watched me.
I knew they were there; you could smell them.

in my adventures I would come across
something magical:

witch hair,
a dead man's beard,
a fairy's web...

then I learned it's a gypsy moth's nest--
caterpillar cocoons poisonous to trees,
including apple trees.

science took over:
a piece of glass and the sun...
burn baby, burn.

She is copper delight

beckoning the forces that be
she strides in harmony,
her gray mop tail curled, carefree.
she peers at you aware
of the shifting light and water
movement, steamy nostrils warming
& her black mane, a clear warning
she'll never be owned--
it wouldn't be right.
she exists as a copper delight
for the midsummer sun.

Frayed Knot

These south winds keep the tides at bay long enough to gather beached seaweed for winter gardens. The gulls are out and about. Local lobster boats part waves as their fattened traps titter and sway - sadly they only earn $2.50 a pound. A strike may evolve this Acadian Day 2013, our yellow star setting beneath the tides of these colonized waters

I carry a bucket containing beached buoys of seaweed, feckless shells, stranded feathers and 'fraid not's – things one doesn't need.

I see a safe place to sit on driftwood by a small fire pit next to a dune; its tall grasses still. A blackbird denizen perches on the tallest strand, appears to be eying the 'fraid not' - maybe for a nest?

I press on homeward. In the distance a smoke shack sends a hint of smoked salmon to linger over the pathway.

The rugged fisher person looks my way dauntingly and lights a cigarette, its glowing tip a burnt ember in the evening sky. We nod 'Hello', or are we nodding 'Bye'? We can live without these things.

I'm Half An Orange

i'm half an orange
and it's ok
I don't know what that means either

resting on the plank floor in the sun-porch
is half an orange--

its rind hangs just below the first step
a single seed that fell outward
lies against my old sneaker
where it will remain, barren
under the desert sun

the ants try to carry it away
but the weight is too much--
they retreat to a crack in the stoop

a bee scans for its fruity sweet spot,
a butterfly meanders about me
like a bored child
and a horsefly taunts me

my citrus fragrant hands
flag it away but it won't go

so I perch like the orange--
one leg dangling over the first step,
leaning on my sneakers
and we become one
in some abstract way.
i'm half an orange
and it's ok...

I don't know what that means either.

In Passing
in memory of Canadian activist poet singer songwriter Willie Dunn

their love for us
never departs
they are there
beating the drum
of our heart

July Friday 13th

no ladders to walk under today

just the watering of gardens.
this heat stills even the bumblebee.

a wet brown paper bag,
sort of a winged butterfly,
stopped blowing in the sea breeze
to sit with me on the swing this morning--
its camouflage working over time.

it's going to be a blazing summer day
with butterflies hiding in flowerbeds,
heavy bird song silence permeating the air,
BBQs collecting spider webs
and trees thirsting for a drink--
their curled-edge leaves make
harbingers of an early fall.

Time

time is here
it is now here
right here
now
time ripens
as is grapples the
fractured hourglass
it is lifting its tongue in wrath

We sat at the café

we sat at the café reading deserted tea leaves as the sun
set shallow legs upon the horizon
& the stars drowned in pools of forgotten wishes.
shall we say we traveled long narrow streets between
windows of sleep like rain swept dreamers
why doesn't God offer a prediction?
overlain by leaves, one leaf clings to the rim.

Wonder boxes

The drive down from Nova Scotia was just as I expected, as the cities became lost in a haze of LED lamps and the person beside you toasted new life with a can of beer. In the days before electric cars and roadside motels with orange and red round patio chairs and the fragrance of chlorinated swimming pools, I remember a little restaurant whose coffee was as strong as the lumber-jacketed people it served; big hands grasping cigarettes that glowed, revealing the faint old tall ships wallpaper and calendar dated 1956. Here is where poetry is born. I told the waitress I was a relative of the old sea Captain Joshua Slocum as she poured me another tea and drew a map of the area.

A poet isn't someone who studies creative writing and teaches it even less. A poet is "there" in that moment - a magical creature whose words become wonder boxes. Daily life is a museum, a room filled with glass thoughts, waiting to shape a manuscript - a fake passport to eternity, entertaining the moment - the life of the party, the saint of high culture. As for myself, I cannot entertain the speeches of ghosts or the copperhead snake peering through those eyes. I'm going to rattle my wonder-boxes and live in the moment. It's a mystery how any of us survive.

Flowers in the Sand

We strolled a pebbled pathway
to a white-walled adobe cafe
with pink curtained windows
where several others listened
to a multi-earinged woman
play her guitar and singing

A white pony-tailed man fluted,
and the spirit of birds chimed in
while she sang the wisdom
of great, age-old mountains
resting on the horizon behind her

It was an Enya moment.

We were being served
a gorgeous feast complete
with Sangria and two wine glasses
and as dusk approached
the waiter lit a million candles

There was no need for words
in this unified landscape
where we were each a shard
of moonlight, each a star in our own night

Then the rosy curtains wafted
as you drew me by the hand
away from the cafe
away to all things silent
but the sound of two hearts
becoming flowers in the sand
on a million moonlit beaches
and pebbled trails

Not That Long Ago

it wasn't too long ago that I realized:

I see more
    with my eyes closed

feel more
    with my fingers stretched out

move like a ballerina
    when tip toeing over beach stones

cry often
    under the soft moonlight

smile suddenly
    when a songbird seizes my attention

it wasn't too long ago:

these open eyes
    recognized world illusions

clenched life
    like it was balled-up barbwire

glared at dances of friendship
    slipping away through time

direction-less
    under moonless nights

the sudden death
    of humanity's heartbeat (sigh)

how is it my blood
    doesn't become spiked iron?

The Blue City

As I stare at Chefchaouen (the blue city)
and its alleys of richly-colored flower pots
pink rose petals flow from my lips,
my eyes release poppies,
remembering a million shades of red,
and these hands vine about my body
as thoughts on a trellis while I begin
the transformation I was born to.

Harry Thurston's eyes
dedicated to poet Harry Thurston

pebbles wash up on the world's shores
safe guarded by archangel Raphael
these pebbles – your eyes –
a coat of many colors:

Atlantic dark

Mediterranean blue

Caribbean green

how I plummeted
into those Thurston oceans
thirsting for Precambrian seas
like an ancient, exotic bird
scanning the untamed horizon
listening to oceans that thunder

on the rocks
your poems echo from
poems echo from
echo from

    f r o m

Peering at the ocean from the Cape

peering at the ocean from the cape
I see you: a dark, rugged pillar
and bear witness
to the sensual curvature of back
pressing firm against your dress,
crowned by a black hat
sea breezes can't pinch.
your crumbling structure, part of
an ancient stone wall,
held no beauty until now.

to your right, an old oak's trunk
has been carved by time's persistent wind,
and I see seasons' weight meted out
in spirit, as you both rise
to greet every day.

while peering at the ocean from the cape
I wonder: has someone left?
your black dress sways and beckons
incoming ships, and silently,
ever so slightly, the oak bows
for a closer look at you,
peering at the ocean
from the cape

Mother
dedicated to my mother

Mother,
your torch
remains aglow
and I
in awe of its light

Go as a River

go as a river, be the keeper of the fallen limb sea   dance,
sun worship in O'Keeffe fluidity dancing bones loving
bones bones of love root into short-lived tides, where
even beach-faced inland spume cannot break down a
river bones resurface bygone lives with unborn ones birth
rhythmic ripples go, go as a river

i am a Pirate

i am a pirate

i cannot say things rightly

'burp, grumble low and snort'

i must say things impolitely

Hunters' moon

cloaked by an orange
and black hunting jacket,
shod by a pair of lace-less old sneakers,
feeling serene and unhurried,
my pocketed hands discover
a prized scotch mint

Three summer haiku

heatwave breeze
and rainbow dreams
underbrush & wildflower

summer morning
a cat snores
among bulrushes

the dreamy field is open
one breath, one budding path
focus on the rose

Three fall haiku

moonlit night
a falling star
among fireflies

buck moon
peeking over pines
my sleepy eye

a whisper shields
the silence of night
breaking through taboo

When I Die

when I die
cast my face--
purse my lips
in a forever kiss
mount them on the mantel,
light a fire and a candle, watch
my shadow dance
when you miss me the most
lay lavender on the ledge,
light a candle and waltz
with me till dawn
try to forgive me
when I die
cast my hand--
place it on the mantel
when it is spring
let dandelions cradle it,
cranberry branches in winter,
beach pebbles with salty grass
in summer and in fall,
a maple leaf ... and
forgive me before you die
take me with you--
place my mask next to yours
place my hand in yours *take me with you*

Weeds

dedicated to my mother

To you I am a weed
plucked daily and discarded
yet my seed manages to soar
with prevailing winds, to rest
on your garden gloves.

You never once look back
to see my heart taking refuge
in thorny Hawthorn trees
where birds of beauty prey.

Their beaks pierce the fragile petals
of broken hearts, blood-letting,
until the naturally slow flow
of death prevails

you reach for your gloves
and dust off the virtues
undiscovered

Wasted No Time

in memory of the late Honorable Pierre Elliott Trudeau

you wasted no time and never wavered
respect flowered like a rose tossed in faith

your sons and daughters aligned strong
along the rails of time--

those petals lined our borders today
as a distantly tolling bell cried out
riveted us all at attention

Spring

I tread gently--
the loose twigs planted last fall
show the rough winter;
they are still waiting.

spring clouds loom and
temperatures drop but
soon the hoary embrace will falter,
warm skies will cling
to everything.

I glance upward, taken in
by a distant blue-jay call.

God, why did you make
their song so distracting?

a twig crunched

"Oops, now I did it!"

-- this twig will no longer bear fruit.

Time-line

dedicated to Beat Poet Laureate Ron Whitehead USA

time-line
I see you there:
a bearded Moses, pondering

CRACK

there was an earthquake
not the kind that defaces
but the kind that awakens

and you
one foot in
one foot out

or is it the other way around
matters not, you walk
this time-line with parting reflections

Taxi

sitting. shaded. waiting.
streetlight red. no vacancy.
sit. alone. red. green. yellow.
black cab.

sha. doe.

sha. de. doe.

Jane-doe. Jane does. arrived.
found. unbound. hands clenched.
worry. has no right.
in. a. sitting. place.

Surrendering

21st Century

sand diamonds glisten by moonlight,
wine-sparkling seas jostle for a kiss...
their rippling tongues nuzzle
the shoreline's sandy neck
and in the eve of night
I am the sand - my lover, the moon

(nearly hidden by a veil of stars)

and the promiscuous sea.
I surrender to night's caressing hand
as, at the waters edge, I drift.

So Far Away, yet

dedicated to poet Jeff Cannon for his inspiration

there yes there right there midst copper paths
snow dreams fall on this cool day
breath flows icy river currents
clearly wildlife wander near
needle imprints shadow
weaving castle forests
not even there, yet, there
yes there right there
stomping Yeats, Keats tha thump   tha thump

Beat poets

nowhere somewhere everywhere
my bones pine to follow their naked path,
be unknotted, enterprising and unafraid - a towering
tamarac or rutting moose, an airy shrub sipping on
epiphanies intoxicated by subtler reflections
(new worlds sprung from old)
from ecstatic revelries aged beyond any primeval wood
or glade.

A beautiful day

sitting on my porch
sipping tea
blue heron fly by
tree leaf petals
fall like confetti

Bridge

I spotted you
beneath the red sun;
shadow of a man
whose smile bridged
the path I was about to take

Sitting at Tim Horton's in Saint Louis

we gather over coffee at Tim Horton's in Saint Louis;
those old friends that time forgot and whose company I
cherish, whose jokes and gossip make the world go
round. I am but a flower keeping company with streaming
brooks.

"watering a flower is time well spent."

I thinking of my late sister: "don't forget to call Vicky",
mom said. I nodded and smiled. "don't forget her
birthday card," mom reminded. After calling and then
signing her card, I cried.

These old friends are destined to become memories too

Sitting at the Computer

sitting at the computer

cold coffee:
blank screen
dried up pen
and people think
being a poet is easy--

I am a statue
made of plaster
and steel rods
whitewash paint
circled by pigeons

sitting at the computer
second coffee cup:
dazed by the screen
inspiration robbed
perspiration gained

"100% humidity today!"
I try to refocus the
impossible task.
blink. think.
whiteout

Shoreline

That night of doubting that you really loved me
thunder sounded. I could hear its drum beat
secluded among stones that rumble during high tide.
"Where are you?" my heart map asks

You carved distant whispers on me that even gypsy gods
couldn't bury so far from home

Pigeon feed
*tribute to uncle Milty, *Canada's Peoples Poet Milton Acorn*

In the early 1980's Canada's Peoples Poet Milton Acorn
and I sat down. Milt said little when we were together on
that bench overlooking the Charlottetown Harbor, where
he left tiny written paper scraps all over -- pigeon feed. I
guess it was his way of giving back to the earth

December 1st 2017

it's a silvery silence,
mud puddled framed reflections,
nearby birches graying,
a stray creamsicle cat
wandering down the lane-way.
he's a victim in this monochrome dream.
a blue-jay speeds past the window, and
I jump, smile, laugh at myself -- it is the only
sound I heard today

Dance naked

dance naked in the rains--
let the puddle below your feet
reflect your spirit, love--

let the springs of your life,
the autumns of your lips,
the maps between your eyes
be routes for the world to follow

dance naked in the sun--
inflame the bosom butterflies
reflect your self, love--
become the desert's mother,
become the winter's princess

    -- a bride to all

Cottage I

the hammers beat the plywood
like a sacred drum.
it's closing time.

up at the cottage
during autumn, when the door closes,
the interior is mummified
like sweet honey wood

and with great remorse
we close the windows
to keep it in.

Cottage II

we love going to the closed-up cottage
in spring. When the door opens
the interior is intoxicating
like sweet honey wood

yet with great remorse
we open windows
and let it out

Chinatown Night Market

"Let's meet under the canopy
Friday at dusk--
      I'll be wearing my hair in a ponytail,
      jeans & your old white shirt…
      dark sunglasses"

your message said.
It's been a hectic week:
      one "if I didn't have bad luck
      I wouldn't have any luck at all", kinda week

I finally made it to Chinatown,
strolled the dozens of multi-colored canopies
      thinking I'd see you as I headed to your place.
      I bought a few things "just in case".

It's nearing 8 pm & my heart weighs heavy:
how I looked forward to tonight, to feel your arm in mine
      strolling under the canopies
      laughing the night away

Instead, I am alone,
standing in everyone's way,
      hoping for a glimpse of you
      somewhere in the crowd.
      Why did you say sunglasses?

Early Saturday morning I grabbed the paper
at a nearby newsstand. With coffee in hand I read:
      Murder at Chinatown Night Market...
      Was it you? I frantically reached for the cell--
      rang, texted, waited

After a sleepless night, headed to the local
coffee shop and there you were.
      who was with you
      did you forget out date

The dark sunglasses rested on the table
beside your full coffee cup.
      You put them on, never looking up.
      I stood in everyone's way
      while you walked past.

Disruptive parallels

an apocalyptic message
hovers in the mist--
placid silver waters skillfully
appeal to the prophet whose
whispers confer sophistry on
parallels across the creek
while gazing across the creek
the wizard lifts a brow
as falling leaves cover all tracks

A Haiku and two Senryu

never alone
the morning rose inflames
a phoenix calling

the camera eye blinks--
dusky patchwork
of shadows

(senryu)

"a rum to order, a cigar to light"
while living the poetic life--
"Goodnight" Hemingway!

(senryu)

Cabin by the creek

you said to meet you
at the cabin by the creek.
I ruffle leaves,
my breath rising.
I become a stovepipe,
black and weathered--
my hands knotted pines
grasping a dew-beaded poppy,
your voice lavender and unapologetic
whispers along the leafy roadway--
my lifelong love,
the poppy is falling

Brick red chair
(ephemeral poem)

where you sat Saturday, before the leaving,
before that last shadow's eve

upon arriving I noticed the broken chair leg
you must have left in fury.

the scooter keys remained on the window ledge.
cobblestones reveal no footprint--
I stand without direction

Blizzard

where is that blizzard?
I have looked everywhere
under tree branches
ice caps
roof tops
beneath snow boots
all I find are scrapings of moon dust

Black swan

inspired by photo of Ava Homa

there you stand
one hand resting
on the wooden fence,
body poised in a
black evening gown,
the ballerina of trees sway;
the earth's heart beats
and you are the lead actress
focused. unmoved.
I photograph you
and then you flutter
your feathers and *soar*

Benjamin Slocum

Captain Joshua Slocum's son

solid like stone
you paddle rapids
as if you were
water yourself

an eagle eye
slow breath
muscles tense
as ragged cliffs

circling birds
break the gaze
and fly west seeking
flights of ghosts

shooting rapids into
the Damariscotta river
in Maine, paddle in hand
and summers well spent

Before nightfall

barren and ragged
cello & violin
weeping willows
dangling straw notes
footpaths to awakened daffodils
vertically set, a last living mirage
before the curtains are drawn

Bass

dedicated to Joan Sanipass

I cast around my aunt's shoreline
(almost froze my mitts off)
threw out my best arsenal:
It's too early yet--
bass are too smart to run
maybe next time

Autumn
dedicated to my dad

Thoughts travel to times when my parents closed up the
cottage, raking leaves, covering windows with weathered
white planked boards, the sound of mom in the kitchen,
cupboard doors slamming, pots and pans clanging, tap on
to drain it so it doesn't freeze and crack through the
winter, fridge spotless...

dad piling leaves and old debris in an old rust   barrel
raccoons have toppled over a dozen times. He is standing
guard over the fire, leaning on a rake pole, grinning
slightly. He loves it here among the leaves and
evergreens, the salt air breezing through his hair. the only
time he never wears a suit.

Ann with an 'E'

she followed me everywhere.

I saw her in window shops peering at me, in newspapers,
posters on telephone poles, wigs on people with eyes in
the back of their heads. I saw her dance on stage, heard
her sing, saw her wink. she was even on TV when I was
with actor Cedric Smith, of "Road to Avonlea" fame--
and she just glared at me so I decided to go red as well,
this was the last straw:
up and down University Ave with "carrot-top" blazing I
went over to Confederation Center, down alleyways to the
Marina and finally to Victoria Park--she was nowhere in
sight!

I found her back at the tourist shops but she was no
longer looking at me or I was invisible, I walked in
through the open door, passed in front of her and she
didn't even blink--freeing me to leave P.E.I.

Salt

don't you like sitting on driftwood
salt whetting your lips
drifting along near naked bodies
lined up like cigars in a sandbox

ever see scavenging gulls
tossing seaweed from great heights
blanketing carcasses
on distant inlets

ever notice burnt driftwood left by partying teens
scraps of crusty burned newspaper
one with a name you recognize
written in the obits

ever feel wild
free as the winds
and gales transforming
shorelines and sandbars

ever sift grains of sand
onto glowing red embers
at the fires edge of driftwood
with seaweed dangling
from its opened armpits

did you ever drift
in the dust of starlight
transcending the sands of time
returning to where you were born

don't you like sitting on drift wood
salt whetting your dreams

Haunter of the seas

it was like it was yesterday:

a hurried brisk squall
underfoot seaweed that lead
I followed
and was taken away
lifted by winds ashore
clouds parted, leading
I followed
watching the sky
with kaleidoscopic eyes
I breathed--
waiting for a sign

www.ingramcontent.com/pod-product-compliance
Lightning Source LLC
Chambersburg PA
CBHW031007090426
42737CB00008B/722